STEAM COOKING

STEAM COOKING

healthy eating from south-east asia with 20 recipes

KIM CHUNG LEE

LORENZ BOOKS

This edition is published by Lorenz Books

This edition is published by Lorenz Books,
an imprint of Anness Publishing Ltd,
Blaby Road, Wigston, Leicestershire LE18 4SE; info@anness.com
www.lorenzbooks.com; www.annesspublishing.com

© Anness Publishing Ltd 2013

A CIP catalogue record for this book is available from the British Library.

PUBLISHER: Joanna Lorenz
MANAGING EDITOR: Linda Fraser
EDITOR: Sarah Uttridge
DESIGNER: Adelle Morris
EDITORIAL READER: Sylvie Venet-Tupy
ADDITIONAL TEXT: Katharine Blakemore
RECIPES: Kit Chan, Yasuko Fukuoka, Shirley Gill, Deh-Ta Hsiung, Kathy Man,
    Sallie Morris, Kate Whiteman.
PHOTOGRAPHY: Nicki Dowey, Amanda Heywood, Janine Hosegood,
    William Lingwood, Thomas Odulate, Craig Robertson

NOTES

Bracketed terms are intended for American readers.

For all recipes, quantities are given in both metric and imperial measures and,
where appropriate, measures are also given in standard cups and spoons.
Follow one set, but not a mixture, because they are not interchangeable.

Standard spoon and cup measures are level.
1 tsp = 5ml, 1 tbsp = 15ml, 1 cup = 250ml|8fl oz

Australian standard tablespoons are 20ml. Australian readers should use 3 tsp
in place of 1 tbsp for measuring small quantities of gelatine, flour, salt, etc.

Medium (US large) eggs are used unless otherwise stated.

APPETIZERS AND SNACKS

MAIN COURSES

SIDE ORDERS

CONTENTS

simply steamed 6
equipment 8
how to use a steamer 10

APPETIZERS AND SNACKS 12
steamed seafood packages 14
spiced scallops in their shells 16
mussels in black bean sauce 18
chicken and sticky rice balls 20
chicken and vegetable bundles 22
mini phoenix rolls 24
aromatic stuffed chillies 26
steamed pork and water chestnut wontons 28

MAIN COURSES 30
sticky rice parcels 32
crispy and aromatic duck 34
steamed eggs with beef and spring onions 36
grey mullet with pork 38
paper-wrapped and steamed red snapper 40
malaysian steamed trout fillets 42
steamed lettuce-wrapped sole with mussels 44
monkfish and scallop skewers 46
pan-steamed mussels with thai herbs 48

SIDE ORDERS 50
steamed flower rolls 52
warm vegetable salad with peanut sauce 54
steamed aubergine with sesame sauce 56
stuffed sweet peppers 58
steamed morning glory with fried garlic and shallots 60
steamed vegetables with chiang mai spicy dip 62

INDEX 64

simply steamed

Steaming is probably the oldest form of cooking in the world. Originally food was cooked using the steam and stones from hot springs. Nowadays a vast array of steaming equipment is available to buy, and there are ways of improvising using a wok or saucepan.

Food is steamed in the moist heat generated by boiling or simmering liquid, without the food touching the liquid. The food is usually placed in or on a perforated container that is raised above the liquid and the container is covered to prevent heat escaping.

THE ASIAN CONNECTION

Steaming is popular in many Asian countries, especially China, where people have been cooking by this method for 3,000 years or more. Steaming has come a long way since then, and is now one of the most popular methods of cooking in the world.

In the Western world steaming was often associated with tasteless food like unseasoned white fish, or stodgy suet puddings. But, through the Asian influence, with its subtle use of flavourings, steamed food has become a much more exciting proposition.

STEAMED VEGETABLES TO DIP

STUFFED SWEET PEPPERS

PAN-STEAMED MUSSELS

WHY STEAM?

It has long been recognized that steaming is one of the healthiest methods of cooking.

Steaming is a very natural way to cook food and it retains moisture, vitamins, nutrients and flavours. Very little fat is needed to steam food, perhaps just a little to stop it sticking or some brushed on top for additional flavour.

Steaming is a moist heat so meat stays tender and does not dry out. Fish remains in one piece and does not fall apart, and vegetables can be steamed until perfectly tender yet still crisp.

Another advantage is that you do not need to give steaming food constant attention. You can attend to other parts of the meal and, if you need food to rest for a while, simply turn off the heat and it will keep warm in the residual heat.

THE BEST FOODS TO STEAM

Almost every vegetable can be steamed. Green vegetables such as broccoli and cabbage cook particularly well – they steam quickly and keep their vivid colour. Root vegetables, such as carrots and potatoes, although taking the same time to cook as when boiled, are much better steamed; they retain their texture and their flavour is not lost.

There is nothing worse than overcooked fish, and steaming is perfect for lightly cooking all different types, from delicate sole fillets to more densely textured tuna or swordfish steaks. Shellfish, which is often bought ready cooked, can be lightly steamed in order to reheat.

When preparing poultry or red meat for steaming, thinly slice, mince (grind) or cut into small even-sized pieces so the food cooks quickly and evenly.

INFORMATION ABOUT THE BOOK

This delightful book takes you through the basics of steaming, explains which steamer to buy and how to use it, then offers three fabulous chapters of recipes inspired by the cooking of China, Japan, Thailand and other South-east Asian countries. There are delicious dim sum, such as pork and water chestnut wontons and chicken and sticky rice balls, which were originally eaten as Chinese street food. The Thai influence, with its use of aromatic herbs and spices, is found in recipes such as pan-steamed mussels, and stuffed sweet (bell) peppers. Japan is represented by recipes for paper-wrapped snapper, and steamed aubergine (eggplant) with sesame sauce. Warm vegetable salad served with a rich peanut sauce is based on the Indonesian recipe, *Gado-Gado*.

equipment

A steamer is a useful addition to any kitchen and there are many types of steamer on the market. Which one you buy should be determined by your needs as well as your budget.

The range of steamers include stacking stainless steel pans, Chinese bamboo baskets, a trivet used with a wok or a little collapsible perforated steamer, which fits inside a pan. Look for them in your local cook shop or department store to decide which one is best for you. Each one has its advantages, and they are described in the following sections.

BAMBOO BASKETS

The Chinese steaming basket is the oldest type of steaming equipment, with examples dating back to ancient China.

The most popular size is about 20cm|8in in diameter, but these baskets can range from 10cm|4in to a whopping 50cm|20in.

The baskets are placed over a pan or wok of boiling water and can be used singly or stacked one upon the other so that several dishes or whole meals can be cooked at once. When using stacked baskets, put the ingredients that need the longest cooking time in the lowest basket. Ingredients that have a strong flavour and that may drip juices should also be in the bottom basket. Foods such as green vegetables, or anything that just needs reheating, should be put into the top basket.

Bamboo baskets are an economical piece of steaming equipment and although the cheapest place to buy one

is a Chinese supermarket, they can also be found in department stores and cooking equipment shops everywhere. Care must be taken when using bamboo baskets as they burn easily.

STAINLESS STEEL STEAMER

Although a stainless steel steamer is probably the most expensive type, it is a good investment if you intend to use a steamer often. It has a lidded, deep outer pan to hold the steaming liquid and one or two perforated inner baskets, which fit snugly inside to hold the food. For the greatest versatility, choose the widest type you can find, with a good, deep base. These steamers are very sturdy and robust. They can be used on any heat source and will last for many years.

BAMBOO BASKETS

PANS AND WOKS

STAINLESS STEEL STEAMER

STEAMING IN A SAUCEPAN

STEAMING IN A BAMBOO BASKET

STEAMING WITH A TRIVET

SAUCEPAN

When using a saucepan to steam, a little improvisation is necessary. To hold the food above the water, you need some kind of heatproof, perforated container, such as a colander or sieve, which can then be covered by the pan lid or foil. You can also use a collapsible stainless steel steamer, which unfolds like the petals of a flower and expands to fit different sizes of pan; these are available from most cook stores.

A heatproof plate, especially a deep, soup-type plate that can rest on the rim of the pan, can be used for cooking small pieces of fish or meat. If cooked on a deep plate any natural juices will be retained and can be used as a sauce. Make sure that you wear heatproof gloves when removing the very hot plate from the pan.

WOK

Although usually thought of as a piece of equipment for stir-frying food at high temperatures, a wok can also be turned into a very effective steamer, by using either a bamboo basket or a trivet, which will sit on the sloping sides of the wok, just above the water level. Choose a bamboo basket, which best fits the size of your wok as they are available in a variety of sizes.

SUCCESSFUL STEAMING IN A WOK USING A BAMBOO STEAMER

1 Put the wok on the stovetop, ensure it is stable, then add about 5cm|2in of water and bring to simmering point.

2 Put the bamboo steamer containing the food into the wok where it will rest on the sloping sides.

3 Cover the basket with its lid and steam for the recommended time. Top up with boiling water, if necessary.

SUCCESSFUL STEAMING IN A WOK USING A TRIVET

1 Place the trivet, which can be either metal or bamboo, into the wok. Pour in enough boiling water to come just below the trivet, then carefully place a heatproof plate holding the food to be steamed on to the trivet.

2 Cover the wok, bring to the boil, then reduce the heat to a simmer and steam for the recommended time, topping up with boiling water if, necessary.

how to use a steamer

STEAMING FISH

To cook fish in a steamer, half fill the base pan with water and bring it to the boil. Reduce the heat until the water simmers. Place the fish into the steamer basket, then cover the fish with grease-proof (waxed) paper. Place the basket into (or on top of) the base pan and cover with a lid or foil, making sure that the basket does not touch the water. The fish will cook very quickly, but do check the water level from time to time and top it up with boiling water from a kettle, if needed.

Unless you have a very large steamer or a fish kettle, a whole fish will probably need to be cut in half before cooking and then re-assembled to serve. Prawns or shrimps need only to be cooked until they turn from grey to pink. Shellfish such as scallops and mussels can be steamed in their shells.

STEAMING VEGETABLES

Vegetables should be cut into even-sized pieces and arranged in one layer in the steamer basket to allow the moist, hot air to circulate around them.

COOKING DIM SUM

Dumplings and savoury buns are very popular Chinese snack foods that can be easily found in the freezer and chilled cabinets in Chinese and Asian supermarkets. To cook them, line a steamer basket with spinach or lettuce leaves, then arrange the dumplings or buns in the basket, allowing room for them to expand when cooked. They will take 8–10 minutes to cook and can be served straight from the steamer, with a sweet or hot dipping sauce.

PERFECT REHEATING

All kinds of foods can be successfully reheated in a steamer, from crêpes and pancakes to ready-cooked vegetables and left-overs.

A steamer is ideal for reheating foods such as the thin pancakes that are served with crispy duck. Buy them ready prepared, either fresh or frozen. To reheat, separate the pancakes and place a square of non-stick baking parchment between each one. Wrap the pancakes in foil and seal securely. Put the foil parcel into the steamer and cook for

STEAMING FISH

STEAMING VEGETABLES

REHEATING FOOD

ADDING FLAVOURINGS

LINING WITH LETTUCE

LINING WITH BANANA LEAVES

3–5 minutes until the pancakes are hot.

A bamboo steamer is ideal for this type of steaming because once the foil and paper are removed, the pancakes can be kept warm and served straight from the steamer basket.

USING FLAVOURINGS, HERBS AND SPICES

All kinds of food can be enhanced by the addition of herbs, spices and flavourings. Tuck lemon slices, fresh herb sprigs or bay leaves around the food, sprinkle whole spices, such as cardamom pods, star anise or peppercorns either over or around the food to impart a subtle flavour, and add flavourings such as lemon grass, fresh ginger or vanilla pods (beans) to the steamer basket so that their flavour is absorbed by the food. Chopped herbs,

crushed garlic, seasoning or ground spices are best sprinkled over the food before steaming.

The cooking liquid underneath the steamer basket can also be flavoured if you like. Add herbs, spices, garlic, stock (bouillon) cubes or wine to the water. Their flavours will not only be absorbed by the food but the wonderful aroma will also fill your kitchen.

Instead of plain vegetable or sunflower oil, rich-tasting olive oil or oils flavoured with chilli, basil or garlic are good, lightly brushed over food that is to be steamed, to add a mild flavour.

The steamer basket can be lined with banana leaves, lotus leaves or even lettuce and spinach. This has several advantages. The leaves not only prevent the food sticking to the steamer, but they also impart a subtle flavour to

the food – and they look very pretty into the bargain.

Don't get carried away, when adding herbs, spices and flavourings to steamed food. Use one or two that complement each other and the food that you are cooking. If you use too many or too much, the flavour will be strong and overpowering.

CAREFUL COOKING

Take extra care when lifting the lid or removing foil from steamers as steam that could cause scalds or burns will be trapped underneath. Always lift the lid away from you.

If you think that the food might stick to the steamer or if the food has a strong flavour that might be absorbed by a bamboo steamer, line the basket with pierced non-stick parchment.

APPETIZERS
AND SNACKS

These little savoury dishes are full of flavour and make a wonderful introduction to an Asian meal. Serve them either as an appetizer with drinks or as a first course. A selection of the little stuffed packages and parcels with their dipping sauces will make a perfect dim sum meal.

steamed seafood packages

Ingredients | SERVES 4

225g|8oz crab meat

50g|2oz shelled prawns (shrimp), chopped

6 water chestnuts, chopped

30ml|2 tbsp chopped bamboo shoots

15ml|1 tbsp chopped spring onions (scallions)

5ml|1 tsp chopped fresh root ginger

15ml|1 tbsp soy sauce

15ml|1 tbsp Thai fish sauce

12 rice sheets

banana leaves

oil, for brushing

15ml|1 tbsp soy sauce

TO GARNISH

2 spring onions (scallions), shredded

2 red chillies, seeded and sliced

fresh coriander (cilantro) leaves

Very neat and delicate, these tasty packages filled with crab meat, prawns and Thai flavourings make an excellent appetizer.

1 Combine the crab meat, chopped prawns, chestnuts, bamboo shoots, spring onions and ginger in a bowl. Mix well, then add the soy sauce and Thai fish sauce. Stir until blended.

2 Take a rice sheet and dip it into warm water. Place it on a clean, flat surface and leave for a few seconds to soften.

3 Place a spoonful of the filling in the centre of the sheet and fold into a square package. Repeat with the rest of the rice sheets and seafood mixture.

4 Line a steamer with banana leaves and brush them with oil. Put the packages, seam side down, on the leaves and steam over a pan of boiling water at a high heat for 6–8 minutes, or until the filling is cooked.

5 Garnish with the shredded spring onions, sliced chillies and coriander, and serve straight from the steamer.

COOK'S TIP The seafood packages will spread out when steamed, so be sure to space them well apart to prevent them from sticking together.

spiced scallops in their shells

Ingredients | SERVES 2

8 scallops, shelled (ask the fishmonger to reserve the cupped side of 4 shells)

2 slices fresh root ginger, shredded

1/2 garlic clove, crushed

2 spring onions (scallions), green parts only, cut into fine strips

salt and ground black pepper

FOR THE SAUCE

1 garlic clove, crushed

15ml|1 tbsp grated fresh root ginger

2 spring onions (scallions), white parts only, chopped

1–2 fresh green chillies, seeded and finely chopped

15ml|1 tbsp light soy sauce

15ml|1 tbsp dark soy sauce

10ml|2 tsp sesame oil

Scallops are excellent steamed, and when served with this spicy sauce, they make a delicious, yet simple, appetizer for four people or a light lunch for two.

1 For each scallop, scrape away the beard-like fringe next to the edible white and orange (coral) part. Remove the intestinal thread.

2 Remove the edible part from the shell and rinse well. Scrub the shells in cold water.

3 Place two scallops in each shell and then season lightly with salt and pepper. Scatter the ginger, garlic and spring onions on top of the scallops.

4 Place in a steamer over a pan of boiling water for about 6 minutes, or until the scallops look opaque (you may have to do this in batches).

5 Meanwhile, make the sauce. Mix together the garlic, ginger, spring onions, chillies, soy sauces and sesame oil. Pour into a small serving bowl.

6 Remove each shell from the steamer, taking care not to spill the juices. Arrange on a serving plate with the sauce bowl in the centre. Serve at once.

mussels in black bean sauce

Ingredients | SERVES 4

15ml|1 tbsp vegetable oil

2.5cm|1in piece of fresh root ginger, finely chopped

2 garlic cloves, finely chopped

1 fresh red chilli, seeded and chopped

15ml|1 tbsp black bean sauce

15ml|1 tbsp dry sherry

5ml|1 tsp caster (superfine) sugar

5ml|1 tsp sesame oil

10ml|2 tsp dark soy sauce

20 cooked New Zealand green-shelled mussels

2 spring onions (scallions), 1 shredded and 1 cut into fine rings

The large, green-shelled mussels from New Zealand are perfect for this delicious dish. If possible, ask your fishmonger for the cooked mussels on the half shell.

1 Heat the vegetable oil in a frying pan or wok. Fry the ginger, garlic and chilli with the black bean sauce for a few seconds. Add the sherry and caster sugar and cook for 30 seconds more.

2 Remove the sauce from the heat and stir in the sesame oil and soy sauce. Mix thoroughly.

3 Have a pan ready with about 5cm|2in of boiling water and a heatproof plate that will fit inside it on a trivet or in a basket

4 Place the mussels in a single layer on the plate then spoon over the black bean sauce to cover them evenly.

5 Sprinkle the spring onions over the mussels, cover the plate tightly with foil and place it in the pan on the trivet or in the basket.

6 Steam the mussels over a high heat for about 10 minutes, or until the mussels have heated through. Serve immediately.

chicken and sticky rice balls

Ingredients | MAKES ABOUT 30

450g|1lb|4 cups minced (ground) chicken

1 egg

15ml|1 tbsp tapioca flour

4 spring onions (scallions), finely chopped

30ml|2 tbsp chopped fresh coriander (cilantro)

30ml|2 tbsp Thai fish sauce

pinch of sugar

225g|8oz cooked glutinous rice

banana leaves

oil, for brushing

ground black pepper

shreds of carrot and red (bell) pepper, and chopped chives, to garnish

sweet chilli sauce, to serve

1 In a mixing bowl, combine the minced chicken, egg, tapioca flour, spring onions and coriander. Mix well and season with Thai fish sauce, sugar and freshly ground black pepper.

2 Spread the cooked sticky rice on a plate or flat tray.

3 Place a teaspoonful of the chicken mixture on the bed of rice. With damp hands, roll and shape the mixture in the rice to make a ball about the size of a walnut. Repeat with the rest of the chicken mixture.

4 Line a steamer with banana leaves and lightly brush them with oil. Place the chicken balls on the leaves, spacing well apart to prevent them sticking together. Steam the chicken balls over a pan of boiling water at a high heat for about 10 minutes, or until cooked.

5 Remove and arrange the chicken balls on serving plates. Garnish with shredded carrots, red pepper and chives. Serve with sweet chilli sauce to dip in.

COOK'S TIP Glutinous rice, also known as sticky rice, has a very high gluten content. It is called sticky rice because the grains stick together when it is cooked. It can be eaten both as a savoury and as a sweet dish.

These delicious rice balls with chicken in the centre make an ideal dinner-party first course as they can be prepared in advance, kept in the refrigerator and steamed just before you are ready to serve. You could garnish the chicken balls in the bamboo steamer and serve with sweet chilli sauce in the centre.

chicken and vegetable bundles

This popular and delicious Chinese snack is extremely easy to prepare in your own kitchen.

Ingredients | SERVES 4

4 skinless, boneless chicken thighs

5ml|1 tsp cornflour (cornstarch)

10ml|2 tsp dry sherry

30ml|2 tbsp light soy sauce

2.5ml|½ tsp salt

large pinch of ground white pepper

4 fresh shiitake mushrooms

1 small carrot

1 small courgette (zucchini)

50g|2oz|½ cup sliced, drained, canned bamboo shoots

1 leek, trimmed

1.5ml|¼ tsp sesame oil

1 Remove any fat from the chicken thighs and cut each lengthways into eight strips. Place the strips in a bowl.

2 Add the cornflour, sherry and 15ml|1 tbsp soy sauce to the chicken. Stir in the salt and pepper and mix well. Cover and marinate for about 10 minutes.

3 Remove and discard the mushroom stalks, then cut each mushroom cap in half (or in slices if very large). Cut the carrot and courgette into eight batons, each about 5cm|2in long, then mix the mushroom halves and bamboo shoots together.

4 Bring a small pan of water to the boil. Add the leek and blanch until soft. Drain thoroughly, then slit the leek down its length. Separate each layer to give eight long strips.

5 Divide the marinated chicken into eight portions. Do the same with the vegetables.

6 Wrap each strip of leek around a portion of chicken and vegetables to make eight neat bundles. Have a pan ready with about 5cm|2in boiling water and a steamer or a heatproof plate that will fit inside the pan on a metal trivet.

7 Place the chicken and vegetable bundles in the steamer or on the plate. Place in the pan, cover with a lid or foil and steam at a high heat for 12-15 minutes, or until the filling is cooked.

8 Meanwhile, mix the remaining soy sauce with the sesame oil. Serve with the chicken and vegetable bundles.

mini phoenix rolls

Lean pork, water chestnuts and Chinese mushrooms
flavoured with fresh ginger make a tasty filling for
omelette rolls. They are ideal as a dinner party first course or a
light lunch, but would also be good for a summer picnic
as they can be served hot or cold.

Ingredients | SERVES 4

2 large (US extra large) eggs, plus
1 egg white

75ml|5 tbsp cold water

5ml|1 tsp vegetable oil

175g|6oz lean pork, diced

75g|3oz|1/2 cup drained, canned
water chestnuts

5cm|2in piece of fresh root ginger, grated

4 dried Chinese mushrooms, soaked in hot
water until soft

15ml|1 tbsp dry sherry

1.5ml|1/4 tsp salt

large pinch of ground white pepper

30ml|2 tbsp rice vinegar

2.5ml|1/2 tsp caster (superfine) sugar

fresh coriander (cilantro) or flat leaf parsley,
to garnish

COOK'S TIP If you like, these
rolls can be prepared a day in
advance, kept in the refrigerator
and steamed just before serving.

1 Lightly beat the two whole eggs
with 45ml|3 tbsp of the water. Heat a
20cm|8in non-stick omelette pan and
brush with a little of the oil. Pour in a
quarter of the egg mixture, swirling
the pan to coat the base lightly. Cook
the omelette until the top is set. Slide
it on to a plate and make three more
omelettes in the same way.

2 Mix the pork and water chestnuts in
a food processor. Add 5ml|1 tsp of the
root ginger. Drain the mushrooms,
chop the caps roughly and add these
to the mixture. Process until smooth.

3 Scrape the pork paste into a
bowl. Stir in the egg white, sherry,
remaining water and salt and pepper.
Mix together thoroughly, cover
and leave in a cool place for
about 15 minutes.

4 Have a pan ready with about
5cm|2in boiling water and a large
heatproof plate that will fit inside it
on a metal trivet. Divide the pork
mixture among the omelettes and
spread into a large square shape in
the centre of each one.

5 Bring the sides of each omelette
over the filling and roll up from the
bottom to the top. Arrange the rolls
on the plate. Cover the plate tightly
with foil and place it in the pan on
the trivet. Steam over a high heat for
about 15 minutes.

6 Make a dipping sauce by mixing the
remaining ginger with the rice vinegar
and sugar in a small dish. Cut the rolls
diagonally in 1cm|1/2in slices, garnish
with the coriander or flat leaf parsley
and serve with the sauce.

aromatic stuffed chillies

Ingredients | SERVES 4-6

10 large fresh green chillies

75g|3oz raw tiger prawns (jumbo shrimp), peeled

115g|4oz lean pork, roughly chopped

15g|¹/₂oz|¹/₂ cup fresh coriander (cilantro) leaves

5ml|1 tsp cornflour (cornstarch)

10ml|2 tsp dry sherry

10ml|2 tsp soy sauce

5ml|1 tsp sesame oil

2.5ml|¹/₂ tsp salt

15ml|1 tbsp cold water

TO GARNISH

1 fresh green chilli, seeded and sliced into rings

1 fresh red chilli, seeded and sliced into rings

cooked peas

This pretty dish is not as fiery as you might expect – so give it a try. Filled with pork and prawns, the chillies make an unusual and tasty start to a meal.

1 Cut the chillies in half lengthways, keeping the stalk intact. Scrape out and discard all of the seeds and set the chillies aside.

2 Make a shallow cut down the centre of the curved back of each prawn. Pull out the black vein with a cocktail stick (toothpick) or your fingers, then rinse the prawn thoroughly.

3 Mix together the pork, prawns and coriander leaves in a food processor. Process the food until smooth.

4 Scrape the mixture into a bowl and mix in the cornflour, sherry, soy sauce, sesame oil, salt and water; cover and leave to marinate for about 10 minutes.

5 Fill each half-chilli with some of the meat mixture. Have a steamer ready or a pan with about 5cm|2in boiling water and a heatproof plate that will fit inside it on a metal trivet.

6 Place the stuffed chillies in the steamer or on the plate, meat side up, and cover with a lid or foil. Steam steadily for 15 minutes, or until the meat filling is cooked. Serve immediately, garnished with the chilli rings and peas.

COOK'S TIP If you prefer a slightly hotter taste, replace half of the green chillies with red ones, and follow the recipe in the same way.

steamed pork and water chestnut wontons

Ingredients | MAKES ABOUT 36

2 large Chinese leaves (Leaves of chinese cabbage), plus extra for lining the steamer

2 spring onions (scallions), finely chopped

1cm | ¹/₂in piece fresh root ginger, chopped

50g | 2oz canned water chestnuts, rinsed and finely chopped

225g | 8oz | 1 cup minced (ground) pork

2.5ml | ¹/₂ tsp Chinese five–spice powder

15ml | 1 tbsp cornflour (cornstarch)

15ml | 1 tbsp light soy sauce

15ml | 1 tbsp Chinese rice wine or dry sherry

10ml | 2 tsp sesame oil

generous pinch of caster (superfine) sugar

about 36 wonton wrappers, each 7.5cm | 3in square

light soy sauce and hot chilli oil for dipping

1 Place the Chinese leaves one on top of the other. Cut them lengthways into quarters and then cut them across into thin shreds.

2 Place the shredded Chinese leaves in a bowl. Add the spring onions, ginger, water chestnuts, pork, Chinese five-spice powder, cornflour and soy sauce.

3 Add the rice wine or the dry sherry, sesame oil and sugar to the mixture and mix well.

4 Place a heaped teaspoon of the filling in the centre of a wonton wrapper. Lightly dampen the edges with water.

5 Lift the wrapper up around the filling, gathering it to form a "purse". Squeeze the wrapper firmly around the middle, then tap the bottom to make a flat base. The top should be open. Place the wonton on a tray and cover with damp kitchen paper. Repeat with the other wonton wrappers until the filling is used up.

6 Line a steamer with Chinese leaves and steam the dumplings over a pan of boiling water for 12–15 minutes, or until they are tender.

7 Remove each batch from the steamer as soon as they are cooked, cover with foil and keep warm. Serve hot with soy sauce and chilli oil for dipping.

These wontons are a favourite afternoon snack in many teahouses in China. If you are expecting guests for afternoon tea, why not bring Asia to your home and serve these little dumplings in the same way, with a large pot of Chinese tea. Your guests will undoubtedly love these small and flavoursome treats.

MAIN
COURSES

Red snapper wrapped in paper, sole steamed
in lettuce leaves and monkfish and scallops
skewered on to lemon grass are just a few of the
spectacular dishes in this chapter. It also includes
the highly aromatic and popular crispy duck and an
unusual and very delicious savoury custard with
beef and spring onions.

sticky rice parcels

Ingredients | SERVES 4

450g | 1lb | 2¼ cups glutinous rice

20ml | 4 tsp vegetable oil

15ml | 1 tbsp dark soy sauce

1.5ml | ¼ tsp Chinese five-spice powder

15ml | 1 tbsp dry sherry

4 skinless, boneless chicken thighs, each cut into 4 pieces

8 dried Chinese mushrooms, soaked in hot water until soft

25g | 1oz dried shrimps, soaked in hot water until soft

50g | 2oz | ½ cup sliced, drained, canned bamboo shoots

300ml | ½ pint | 1¼ cups chicken stock

10ml | 2 tsp cornflour (cornstarch)

15ml | 1 tbsp cold water

4 lotus leaves, soaked in warm water until soft

salt and ground white pepper

1 Rinse the glutinous rice until the water runs clear, then leave in water to soak for 2 hours. Drain and stir in 5ml | 1 tsp of the oil and 2.5ml | ½ tsp salt. Line a large steamer with a piece of clean muslin (cheesecloth).

2 Transfer the rice into the lined steamer. Cover with the lid and steam over boiling water for about 45 minutes, stirring the rice from time to time and topping up the water if needed.

3 Mix together the soy sauce, five-spice powder and sherry. Put the chicken pieces in a bowl, add the marinade and stir to coat. Cover and leave to marinate for 20 minutes.

4 Drain the Chinese mushrooms, cut out and discard the stems, then chop the caps roughly. Drain the dried shrimps. Heat the remaining oil in a non-stick frying pan or wok. Stir-fry the chicken for 2 minutes, then add the mushrooms, shrimps, bamboo shoots and stock. Simmer for 10 minutes.

5 Mix the cornflour to a paste with the cold water. Add the mixture to the pan and cook, stirring, until the sauce has thickened. Add salt and white pepper to taste. Lift the cooked rice out of the steamer and let it cool slightly.

6 With lightly dampened hands, divide the rice into four equal portions. Put half of one portion into the centre of one of the lotus leaves.

7 Spread the rice into a round and place a quarter of the chicken mixture on top. Cover with the remaining half portion of rice. Fold the leaf around the filling to make a neat rectangular parcel. Make three more parcels in the same way.

8 Prepare a steamer. Put the rice parcels, seam side down, into the steamer. Cover with the lid and steam over a pan of boiling water at a high heat for about 30 minutes. Serve the parcels at once on a heated plate.

crispy and aromatic duck

Ingredients | SERVES 6-8

1.8–2.5kg|4–5½lb oven-ready duckling

10ml|2 tsp salt

5–6 whole star anise

15ml|1 tbsp Sichuan peppercorns

5ml|1 tsp cloves

2–3 cinnamon sticks

3–4 spring onions (scallions)

3–4 slices fresh root ginger, unpeeled

75–90ml|5–6 tbsp Chinese rice wine or dry sherry

vegetable oil, for deep-frying

TO SERVE

lettuce leaves

20–24 thin pancakes

120ml|4fl oz|½ cup duck sauce

6–8 spring onions (scallions), cut into fine strips

½ cucumber, cut into fine strips

1 Remove the wings from the duck. Using a large knife, split the body in half down the length of the backbone.

2 Rub salt all over the two duck halves, taking care to rub it in well.

3 Place the duck in a dish with the star anise, peppercorns, cloves, cinnamon, spring onions, ginger and rice wine or dry sherry. Marinate for at least 4–6 hours.

4 Place the duck with the marinade in a steamer positioned in a wok partly filled with boiling water, and steam vigorously for 3–4 hours (longer if possible), topping up the water as necessary.

5 Remove the duck from the cooking liquid and allow to cool for at least 5–6 hours. It must be completely cool and dry or the skin will not crisp.

6 Heat the oil in a preheated wok until smoking, place the duck pieces in the oil, skin side down, and deep-fry for 5–6 minutes, or until crisp and brown, turning just once at the very last moment.

7 Remove the duck pieces from the wok and drain. Take the meat off the bone and place on a bed of lettuce leaves. To serve, wrap a portion of duck in each pancake with a little sauce, spring onion and cucumber. Eat with your fingers.

Because this dish is often served with pancakes, spring onions, cucumber and duck sauce, many people mistakenly think this is Peking Duck. This recipe, however, involves steaming the duck rather than oven cooking. The result is just as crispy, and the delightful aroma makes this dish particularly distinctive. Plum sauce may be substituted for the duck sauce.

steamed eggs with beef and spring onions

Ingredients | SERVES 4–6

115g|4oz sirloin or rump steak
5ml|1 tsp grated fresh root ginger
15ml|1 tbsp Thai fish sauce
3 eggs
120ml|4fl oz|½ cup chicken stock or water
30ml|2 tbsp chopped spring onions (scallion)
15ml|1 tbsp vegetable oil
2 garlic cloves, finely sliced
ground black pepper

This is a very delicate dish from Thailand. You can add less liquid for a firmer custard, but cooked this way it is soft and silky. Other types of meat or seafood can be used instead of beef.

1 Finely chop the beef and place in a large bowl. Add the ginger, Thai fish sauce and black pepper.

2 Beat the eggs together with the stock. Stir into the beef, add the spring onions and beat until well blended. Try to avoid making too many bubbles.

3 Pour the mixture into individual ramekins or a heatproof bowl. Place in a steamer and steam over a pan of boiling water at a gentle heat for 15 minutes, or until the custard is set.

4 Meanwhile, gently heat the oil in a small frying pan. Add the garlic slices and fry for about 2 minutes until just turning golden.

5 Pour the finely sliced garlic and oil over the egg custards. Allow to cool slightly before serving.

VARIATION The Japanese make a different version of this recipe. Simply replace the meat with prawns (shrimp) and the vegetables with spinach and shiitake mushrooms.

grey mullet with pork

Ingredients | SERVES 4

1 grey mullet or snapper, about 900g|2lb, gutted and cleaned

50g|2oz lean pork

3 dried Chinese mushrooms, soaked in hot water until soft

2.5ml|½ tsp cornflour (cornstarch)

30ml|2 tbsp light soy sauce

15ml|1 tbsp vegetable oil

15ml|1 tbsp finely shredded fresh root ginger

15ml|1 tbsp shredded spring onion (scallion)

salt and ground black pepper

sliced spring onion, to garnish

cooked white rice, to serve

This unusual combination of mullet with a pork and mushroom filling makes a spectacular main dish with little effort.

1 Make four diagonal cuts on either side of the fish and rub with a little salt; place the fish in a large shallow heatproof serving dish.

2 Cut the pork into thin strips. Place in a bowl. Drain the soaked mushrooms, remove and discard the stalks and slice the caps thinly.

3 Add the mushrooms to the pork with the cornflour and 5ml|1 tbsp soy sauce. Add 5ml|1 tsp of the oil and a generous grinding of black pepper and mix together.

4 Arrange the pork mixture along the length of the fish. Scatter the ginger shreds over the top.

5 Cover the fish loosely with foil. Have a large roasting pan ready, with about 5cm|2in boiling water, that is large enough to fit the heatproof dish on a metal trivet. Place the dish in the roasting pan, cover and steam over a high heat for 15 minutes.

6 Test the fish by pressing the flesh gently. If it comes away from the bone with a slight resistance, the fish is cooked. Carefully pour away any excess liquid from the dish.

7 Heat the remaining oil in a small pan. When it is hot, fry the shredded spring onion for a few seconds, then pour it over the fish, taking care as it will splatter. Drizzle with the remaining soy sauce, garnish with the spring onion slices and serve with the rice.

paper-wrapped and steamed red snapper

Originally, this elegant Japanese dish featured a whole red snapper wrapped in layered hand-made paper soaked in sake and tied with ribbons. This version is a little easier.

Ingredients | SERVES 4

4 small red snapper fillets, no larger than 6 x 18cm|2½ x 7in snappers

8 asparagus spears, hard ends discarded

4 spring onions (scallions)

60ml|4 tbsp sake

grated rind of ½ lime

½ lime, thinly sliced

salt

1 Sprinkle the red snapper fillets with salt on both sides and chill in the refrigerator for 20 minutes. Preheat the oven to 180°C|350°F|Gas 4.

2 To make the parcels, lay baking parchment measuring 30 x 38cm| 12 x 15in on a work surface. Use two pieces for extra thickness. Fold up one-third of the paper and turn back 1cm| ½in from one end to make a flap.

3 Fold 1cm|½in in from the other end to make another flap. Fold the top edge down to fold over the first flap. Interlock the two flaps to form a long rectangle.

4 At each end, fold the top corners down diagonally, then fold the bottom corners up to meet the opposite folded edge to make a triangle. Press the paper flat with your palm. Repeat the process to make four parcels.

5 Cut 2.5cm|1in from the tips of the asparagus, and slice in half lengthways. Slice the asparagus stems and spring onions diagonally. Par-boil the tips for 1 minute in lightly salted water and drain. Set aside.

6 Open the parcels. Place the asparagus and spring onion slices inside. Sprinkle with salt and place the fish on top. Add more salt, some sake and the lime rind. Refold the parcels.

7 Pour hot water from a kettle into a deep roasting pan fitted with a wire rack so that the water is 1cm|½in below the rack. Place the parcels on the rack. Cook in the centre of the preheated oven for 20 minutes. Unfold a parcel from one triangular side to ensure the fish is white and cooked.

8 Transfer to serving plates. Open the parcels and garnish with lime slices and asparagus tips. Serve at once.

malaysian steamed trout fillets

This simple dish can be prepared extremely quickly, and is suitable for any fish fillets. Serve on a bed of noodles accompanied by ribbons of colourful vegetables.

Ingredients | SERVES 4

8 pink trout fillets of even thickness, about 115g|4oz each, skinned

45ml|3 tbsp grated creamed coconut, or desiccated (dry unsweetened shredded) coconut

grated rind and juice of 2 limes

45ml|3 tbsp chopped fresh coriander (cilantro)

15ml|1 tbsp sunflower or groundnut (peanut) oil

2.5–5ml|1/2–1 tsp chilli oil

salt and ground black pepper

lime slices, to garnish

coriander sprigs, to garnish

cooked noodles, to serve

1 Cut four rectangles of baking parchment, about twice the size of the trout fillets.

2 Place a fish fillet on each piece of the baking parchment and season lightly with salt and pepper.

3 Mix together the coconut, lime rind and chopped coriander and spread a quarter of the mixture over each trout fillet. Sandwich another trout fillet on top of each one.

4 Mix the lime juice with the oils, adjusting the quantity of chilli oil to your own taste. Drizzle over the trout.

5 Fold up the edges of the baking parchment rectangles and pleat them over the trout to make parcels, ensuring that they are well sealed.

6 Place the parcels in a steamer, cover with a lid and steam over a pan of boiling water for about 10–15 minutes, depending on the thickness of the trout fillets. Open the parcels a little to check that the fish is cooked. If not, put back in the oven for another few minutes, making sure that the parcels are closed securely.

7 Transfer the fish and any juices to warmed serving plates. Garnish with the lime slices and coriander sprigs and serve at once with the noodles.

VARIATION As an alternative serving suggestion, leave the trout in their paper packages. Transfer each one to a warmed serving dish and allow your family or friends to eat the fish straight from the paper – somehow it always tastes better that way.

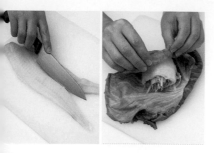

steamed lettuce-wrapped
sole with mussels

If you can afford it, use Dover sole fillets for this recipe; if
not, lemon sole, trout, plaice and brill are all excellent
alternatives and are delicious steamed.

Ingredients | SERVES 4

2 large sole fillets, skinned

12 large fresh mussels

15ml|1 tbsp sesame seeds

15ml|1 tbsp sunflower or groundnut
(peanut) oil

10ml|2 tsp sesame oil

2.5cm|1in piece fresh root ginger, peeled
and grated

3 garlic cloves, finely chopped

15ml|1 tbsp soy sauce or Thai fish sauce

juice of 1 lemon

2 spring onions (scallions), thinly sliced

8 large soft lettuce leaves

1 Cut the sole fillets in half lengthways. Season and set aside. Prepare a steamer. Scrub the mussels and scrape away any beards using a sharp knife. Discard any that are broken or remain open when tapped sharply. Set aside.

2 Heat a heavy frying pan until hot. Toast the sesame seeds lightly but do not allow them to burn. Set aside in a bowl until required.

3 Heat the oils in the frying pan over a medium heat. Add the ginger and garlic and cook until lightly coloured. Stir in the soy sauce or Thai fish sauce, lemon juice and spring onions. Off the heat, stir in the toasted sesame seeds.

4 Lay the pieces of fish on some baking parchment, skinned side up; spread each evenly with the ginger mixture.

5 Roll up each piece of fish, starting at the tail end, then transfer to a baking sheet.

6 Plunge the lettuce leaves into the boiling water you have prepared for the steamer and immediately lift them out with tongs or a slotted spoon. Lay the leaves out flat on kitchen paper and gently pat them dry. Wrap each sole parcel in two lettuce leaves, making sure that the filling is well covered to keep it in place.

7 Arrange the fish parcels in a steamer. Cover and steam over a pan of boiling water for 8 minutes. Add the mussels and steam for 2–4 minutes more, or until opened. Discard any that remain closed. Put the parcels on individual warmed plates, garnish with mussels and serve at once.

monkfish and scallop skewers

Ingredients | SERVES 4

450g|1lb monkfish fillet

8 lemon grass stalks

30ml|2 tbsp fresh lemon juice

15ml|1 tbsp olive oil

15ml|1 tbsp finely chopped fresh coriander (cilantro)

2.5ml|½ tsp salt

large pinch of ground black pepper

12 large shelled scallops, halved crossways

fresh coriander leaves, to garnish

cooked white rice, to serve

Using lemon grass stalks as skewers imbues the seafood with a subtle citrus flavour and makes them more attractive to serve.

VARIATION Raw tiger prawns (shrimp) and salmon make excellent alternative ingredients for the skewers, with or without the monkfish.

1 Remove any membrane from the fish, then cut into 16 large chunks.

2 Remove the outer leaves from the lemon grass to leave thin rigid stalks. Chop the tender parts of the lemon grass leaves finely and place in a bowl. Stir in the lemon juice, oil, chopped coriander, salt and pepper.

3 Thread the fish and scallop chunks alternately on the eight lemon grass stalks. Arrange the skewers of fish and shellfish in a shallow dish and pour over the marinade.

4 Cover and leave in a cool place for 1 hour, turning occasionally. Have a steamer or pan ready with about 5cm|2in boiling water and a large heatproof dish that will fit inside it on a metal trivet or a bamboo streamer.

5 Transfer the skewers to the dish or bamboo steamer, cover with a lid or foil and steam over boiling water for about 10 minutes, or until just cooked. Garnish the skewers with the coriander leaves, and serve with the rice and some cooking juice poured over.

pan-steamed mussels
with thai herbs

Like so many Thai recipes, this is a very easy dish to prepare.
The lemon grass and kaffir lime leaves add a refreshing,
zesty tang to the mussels.

Ingredients | SERVES 4-6

1kg|2¹/₄lb fresh mussels

2 lemon grass stalks, finely chopped

4 shallots, chopped

4 kaffir lime leaves, coarsely torn

2 fresh red chillies, sliced

15ml|1 tbsp Thai fish sauce

30ml|2 tbsp fresh lime juice

thinly sliced spring onions (scallions) and
coriander (cilantro) leaves, to garnish

1 Scrub the mussels and scrape off the beards using a small, sharp knife. Discard any mussels that are broken or which do not close when tapped sharply.

2 Place the mussels in a large, heavy pan and add the lemon grass, shallots, kaffir lime leaves, chillies, Thai fish sauce and lime juice. Mix well.

3 Cover the pan tightly with a lid and steam the mussels over a high heat, shaking the pan occasionally, for 5-7 minutes, or until the shells have opened.

4 Using a slotted spoon, transfer the cooked mussels to a warmed serving dish or individual bowls. Discard any mussels that have failed to open.

5 Garnish the mussels with the thinly sliced spring onions and coriander leaves. Serve at once.

COOK'S TIP It cannot be stressed enough how careful you need to be when cooking seafood. Don't be put off though – just make sure that the mussels are cleaned and de-bearded, and discard any that have not opened during cooking.

SIDE
ORDERS

As well as an accompaniment to a main course these recipes with their interesting preparations of vegetables make excellent vegetarian main courses. This chapter includes delicious warm vegetable salad accompanied by peanut sauce, aubergine with sesame sauce that can be served both hot or cold, and morning glory with fried garlic and shallots.

steamed flower buns

Ingredients | MAKES 16

1 garlic glove, crushed
15ml|1 tbsp oil
110g|4oz roast pork, very finely chopped
1 spring onion, chopped
20ml|1 tsp yellow bean sauce, crushed
2½ml|½ tsp cornflour mixed to a paste with water
fresh chives, to garnish

FOR THE DOUGH
5ml|1 tsp sugar
about 300ml|½ pint|1¼ cups warm water
25ml|1½ tbsp dried yeast
450g|1lb|4 cups strong white bread flour
5ml|1 tsp salt
15g|½oz|1 tbsp lard or white cooking fat
15ml|1 tbsp sesame oil

These attractive little buns are excellent as an accompaniment to a main meal or they can be filled and eaten as a tasty snack.

1 To make the dough, dissolve the sugar in half the water. Sprinkle in the yeast. Stir well, leave for 15 minutes until frothy.

2 Sift the flour and salt into a bowl and rub in the lard. Stir in the yeast mixture with enough of the remaining water to make a soft dough.

3 Knead the dough for 10 mins. Move to an oiled bowl and cover. Leave in a warm place for 1 hour.

4 Knock back (punch down) the dough and divide in two. Divide one piece in half and roll each into a rectangle measuring 30 x 20cm|6 x 8in. Brush the surface of one with sesame oil and lay the other on top. Roll up from the short side and cut into eight rolls.

5 Take each spiral in turn and press down firmly on the rolled side with a chopstick on a clean work surface.

6 Pinch the opposite ends of each roll with the fingers of both hands, then pull the ends underneath and seal.

7 Place the buns on slashed baking parchment in a steamer and leave to double in size.

8 To make stuffed flower buns, first prepare the filling. Fry the garlic in oil until golden, then add the remaining ingredients.

9 Divide the remaining dough into eight pieces. Roll out each piece to a 7.5cm/3-4in round. Place a spoonful of filling in the centre of each, gather up the sides and twist the top to seal. Secure with string. Place in a steamer and leave to double in size.

10 Steam the buns over a pan of rapidly boiling water for 30–35 minutes. Serve hot, garnished with the chives.

warm vegetable salad with peanut sauce

Ingredients | SERVES 2-4

8 new potatoes

225g|8oz broccoli, cut into small florets

225g|8oz|1½ cups fine green beans

2 carrots, cut into thin ribbons with a vegetable peeler

1 red (bell) pepper, seeded and cut into strips

115g|4oz|½ cup sprouted beans

sprigs of watercress or rocket (arugula), to garnish

FOR THE SAUCE

15ml|1 tbsp sunflower oil

1 bird's-eye chilli, seeded and sliced

1 garlic clove, crushed

5ml|1 tsp ground coriander

5ml|1 tsp ground cumin

60ml|4 tbsp crunchy peanut butter

75ml|5 tbsp water

15ml|1 tbsp dark soy sauce

1cm|½in piece fresh root ginger, finely grated

5ml|1 tsp dark brown sugar

15ml|1 tbsp lime juice

60ml|4 tbsp coconut milk

Based on the classic Indonesian recipe, *Gado-Gado*, this salad features raw red pepper and sprouted beans – a crunchy contrast to the warm steamed broccoli, green beans and carrots.

1 First make the peanut sauce. Heat the oil in a pan, add the chilli and garlic, and cook for 1 minute, or until softened. Add the spices and cook for 1 minute. Stir in the peanut butter and water, then cook for 2 minutes, or until combined, stirring constantly.

2 Add the soy sauce, ginger, sugar, lime juice and coconut milk. Cook over a low heat until smooth and heated through, stirring frequently. Transfer to a bowl.

3 Bring a pan of lightly salted water to the boil, add the potatoes and cook for 10-15 minutes, or until tender. Drain, then halve or thickly slice the potatoes, depending on their size.

4 Meanwhile, steam the broccoli and green beans over a pan of boiling water for 4-5 minutes, or until tender but still crisp.

5 Add the carrots to the steamer 2 minutes before the end of the cooking time.

6 Arrange the cooked vegetables on a serving platter with the red pepper strips and sprouted beans. Garnish with watercress or rocket and serve immediately with the peanut sauce.

VARIATION Try topping this salad with slices of warm, hard-boiled egg to make a substantial main course.

steamed aubergine with sesame sauce

Ingredients | SERVES 4

2 large aubergines (eggplant)

400ml|14fl oz|1²/₃ cups water mixed with 5ml|1 tsp dashi-no-moto (dashi stock granules)

25ml|1¹/₂ tbsp caster (superfine) sugar

15ml|1 tbsp shoyu

15ml|1 tbsp sesame seeds

15ml|1 tbsp sake

15ml|1 tbsp cornflour (cornstarch)

salt

FOR THE VEGETABLES

130g|4¹/₂oz shimeji mushrooms

115g|4oz fine green beans

100ml|3¹/₂fl oz|scant ¹/₂ cup water mixed with 5ml|1 tsp dashi-no-moto

25ml|1¹/₂ tbsp caster (superfine) sugar

15ml|1 tbsp sake

1.5ml|¹/₄ tsp salt

dash of shoyu

This autumn recipe from Japan represents a typical Zen temple cooking style: fresh, seasonal vegetables cooked with care. This dish is also delicious cold.

1 Peel the aubergines and cut in quarters lengthways. Prick all over with a skewer, then plunge into salted water for 30 minutes.

2 Drain and steam the aubergines in a steamer over a pan of boiling water for 20 minutes, or until soft. If the quarters are too long to fit in the steamer, cut them in half.

3 Mix the water and dashi-no-moto, sugar, shoyu and 1.5ml/¹/₄ tsp salt together in a large pan. Gently transfer the aubergines to this pan, then cover and cook over a low heat for a further 15 minutes.

4 Grind the sesame seeds finely using a pestle and mortar. Take a few tablespoonfuls of stock from the pan and mix with the ground sesame seeds. Add this mixture to the pan with the aubergines.

5 Thoroughly mix the sake with the cornflour, add to the pan and shake the pan gently but quickly. When the sauce becomes quite thick, remove the pan from the heat.

6 While the aubergines are cooking, prepare and cook the accompanying vegetables. Wash the mushrooms and cut off the hard base part. Separate the large block into smaller chunks with your fingers. Trim the green beans and cut in half.

7 Mix the water and dashi-no-moto, with the sugar, sake, salt and shoyu in a shallow pan.

8 Add the green beans and mushrooms to the sauce and cook for 7 minutes, or until just tender. Serve the aubergines and their sauce in individual bowls with the accompanying vegetables over the top.

stuffed sweet peppers

This is an unusual recipe in that the stuffed
peppers are steamed rather than baked, but the result
is beautifully light and tender. The filling incorporates typical
Thai ingredients like red curry paste, kaffir lime
leaves and fish sauce.

Ingredients | SERVES 4

3 garlic cloves, finely chopped

2 coriander (cilantro) roots, finely chopped

400g|14oz|5$\frac{1}{2}$ cups mushrooms, quartered

5ml|1 tsp Thai red curry paste

1 egg, lightly beaten

15ml|1 tbsp Thai fish sauce

15ml|1 tbsp light soy sauce

2.5ml|$\frac{1}{2}$ tsp sugar

3 kaffir lime leaves, finely chopped

4 yellow (bell) peppers, halved lengthways
and seeded

1 In a mortar or spice grinder, pound
or blend the garlic with the coriander
roots. Scrape into a bowl.

2 Put the mushrooms in a food
processor and pulse briefly until they
are finely chopped. Add to the garlic
mixture, then stir in the red curry
paste, egg, Thai and soy sauces, sugar
and lime leaves.

3 Spoon the mixture loosely into
the pepper halves. Do not pack the
mixture down tightly or the filling
will dry out too much.

4 Place the stuffed pepper halves in
a single layer in a steamer. Cover the
steamer with a lid, then place over a
pan of boiling water. Lower the heat
to a simmer. Steam the peppers for
about 15 minutes, or until the flesh
is soft and tender. Transfer the
peppers to side plates and serve
at once.

VARIATIONS Use whichever colour
of pepper you prefer. All will work
equally well, but the orange and red
ones are sweeter than the green
variety which is slightly bitter.

steamed morning glory with fried garlic and shallots

Morning glory goes by various names, including water spinach, water convolvulus and swamp cabbage. It is a green, leafy vegetable with long-jointed stems and arrow-shaped leaves. The stems remain crunchy while the leaves wilt like spinach when cooked.

Ingredients | SERVES 4

2 bunches morning glory, total weight about 250g|9oz

30ml|2 tbsp vegetable oil

4 shallots, thinly sliced

6 large garlic cloves, thinly sliced

coarse sea salt

1.5ml|1/4 tsp dried chilli flakes

1 Trim and coarsely chop the morning glory into 2.5cm|1in lengths.

2 Place the morning glory in a steamer, cover and steam over a pan of boiling water for about 30 seconds, or until just wilted. If necessary, cook it in batches.

3 Place the green leaves in a bowl or spread out on a large serving plate.

4 Heat the oil in a wok and stir-fry the shallots and garlic over a medium-high heat until golden.

5 Spoon the shallots and the garlic in the oil over the morning glory.

6 Season the morning glory with a little sea salt and sprinkle over the chilli flakes. Divide the greens between four serving plates and serve at once.

VARIATIONS You could use spinach as an equally nutritious replacement for the morning glory. Other substitutes include young spring greens (collards), sprouting broccoli and Swiss chard.

steamed vegetables with chiang mai spicy dip

Ingredients | SERVES 4

1 head broccoli, divided into florets

30g|4¹/₂oz green beans, trimmed

¹/₂ head cauliflower, divided into florets

8 baby corn cobs

30g|4¹/₂oz mangetouts (snow peas) or sugar snap peas

salt

FOR THE DIP

1 fresh green chilli, seeded

4 garlic cloves, peeled

4 shallots, peeled

2 tomatoes, halved

5 pea aubergines (eggplant)

30ml|2 tbsp lemon juice

30ml|2 tbsp soy sauce

2.5ml|¹/₂ tsp salt

5ml|1 tsp sugar

1 Place the broccoli, green beans and cauliflower in a steamer, cover and steam over a pan of boiling water for 4–5 minutes, or until just tender but still with a little "bite".

2 Transfer to a bowl and add the corn cobs and mangetouts or sugar snap peas. Season to taste with a little salt. Toss to mix, then set aside.

3 To make the dip, preheat the grill (broiler) and then wrap the chillies, garlic cloves, shallots, tomatoes and aubergines in foil to make a package. Grill (broil) for about 10 minutes, until the vegetables have softened, turning the package over once or twice during cooking.

4 Unwrap the foil and tip its contents into a mortar or food processor. Add the lemon juice, soy sauce, salt and sugar. Pound with a pestle or process to a fairly liquid paste.

5 Scrape the dip into a serving bowl or four individual bowls. Serve surrounded by the steamed and raw vegetables.

VARIATIONS Use a combination of other vegetables. Steam asparagus instead of beans, or pak choi (bok choy) instead of cauliflower.

COOK'S TIP Cauliflower varieties with pale green curds have a more delicate flavour than those with white curds.

In Thailand, steamed and raw vegetables are often combined to create the contrasting textures that are an essential feature of the national cuisine. By happy coincidence, it is an extremely healthy way to serve them.

INDEX

aubergine, steamed, with sesame
   sauce, 56

beef, steamed eggs
   with spring onions, 36

chiang mai spicy dip, steamed
   vegetables with, 63
chicken and sticky
   rice balls, 21
chicken and vegetable bundles, 22
chillies, aromatic stuffed, 26

duck, crispy and aromatic, 35

eggs, steamed, with beef and spring
   onions, 36

fish: grey mullet with pork, 39
   Malaysian steamed
      trout fillets, 43
   monkfish and scallop skewers, 47
   paper-wrapped and steamed
      red snapper, 40
   steamed lettuce-wrapped sole
      with mussels, 44
flower rolls, steamed, 52

grey mullet with pork, 39

mini phoenix rolls, 25
monkfish and scallop skewers, 47

morning glory, steamed, with fried garlic
   and shallots, 60
mussels in black bean sauce, 18
mussels, pan-steamed, with
   Thai herbs, 48
mussels, steamed lettuce-wrapped
   sole with, 44

peppers, sweet, stuffed, 59
pork: aromatic stuffed chillies, 26
   grey mullet with, 39
   mini phoenix rolls, 25
   steamed pork and water
      chestnut wontons, 29

red snapper, paper-wrapped and
   steamed, 40
rice dishes: chicken and sticky
   rice balls, 21
   sticky rice parcels, 32
rolls, steamed flower, 52

salad, warm vegetable, with
   peanut sauce, 55
scallop skewers, monkfish and, 47
scallops, spiced, in
   their shells, 17
seafood packages, steamed, 14
shellfish: aromatic
   stuffed chillies, 26
   mussels in black
      bean sauce, 18

mussels, steamed lettuce-wrapped
   sole with, 44
pan-steamed mussels with
   Thai herbs, 48
scallop skewers, monkfish and, 47
spiced scallops in their shells, 17
steamed seafood packages, 14
sole, steamed lettuce-wrapped,
   with mussels, 44
sticky rice parcels, 32
sweet peppers, stuffed, 59

trout, malaysian steamed fillets, 43

vegetables: steamed vegetables
   with chiang mai spicy dip, 63
vegetable bundles,
   chicken-wrapped, 22

warm vegetable salad
   with peanut sauce, 55
water chestnut wontons,
   steamed pork and, 29